A Note to Paren

DK READERS is a compelling program for beginning readers, designed in conjunction with leading literacy experts, including Dr. Linda Gambrell, Professor of Education at Clemson University. Dr. Gambrell has served as President of the National Reading Conference and the College Reading Association, and has recently been elected to serve as President of the International Reading Association.

Beautiful illustrations and superb full-color photographs combine with engaging, easy-to-read stories to offer a fresh approach to each subject in the series. Each DK READER is guaranteed to capture a child's interest while developing his or her reading skills, general knowledge, and love of reading.

The five levels of DK READERS are aimed at different reading abilities, enabling you to choose the books that are exactly right for your child:

Pre-level 1: Learning to read
Level 1: Beginning to read
Level 2: Beginning to read alone
Level 3: Reading alone
Level 4: Proficient readers

The "normal" age at which a child begins to read can be anywhere from three to eight years old. Adult participation through the lower levels is very helpful for providing encouragement, discussing storylines, and sounding out unfamiliar words.

No matter which level you select, you can be sure that you are helping your child learn to read, then read to learn!

LONDON, NEW YORK, MELBOURNE,
MUNICH AND DELHI

For Dorling Kindersley
Editor Lucy Dowling
Designer Dan Bunyan
Managing Editor Catherine Saunders
Art Director Lisa Lanzarini
Publishing Manager Simon Beecroft
Category Publisher Alex Allan
Production Editor Siu Yin Chan
Production Controller Nick Seston

For LucasFilm
Executive Editor Jonathan W. Rinzler
Art Director Troy Alders
Keeper of the Holocron Leland Chee
Director of Publishing Carol Roeder
Reading Consultant
Linda B. Gambrell, Ph.D.

First published in the United States in 2010
by DK Publishing
375 Hudson Street, New York, New York 10014

11 12 13 14 10 9 8 7 6 5 4

Published in Great Britain by Dorling Kindersley Limited

DK books are available at special discounts when purchased in bulk
for sales promotions, premiums, fundraising, or educational use.
For details, contact:
DK Publishing Special Markets
375 Hudson Street
New York, New York 10014
SpecialSales@dk.com

A catalog record for this book is available
from the Library of Congress.

ISBN: 978-0-7566-5775-8 (Paperback)
ISBN: 978-0-7566-5776-5 (Hardcover)

Color reproduction by Alta Images
Printed and bound in China by L.Rex

Discover more at

www.dk.com

www.starwars.com

DK READERS

BEGINNING TO READ ALONE
2

STAR WARS

THE CLONE WARS

Stand Aside—
Bounty Hunters!

Written by Simon Beecroft

Cad Bane is perhaps one of the most feared bounty hunters in the galaxy.

He steals valuable objects.
He takes prisoners by force.
He even threatens his captives.

Bounty Hunters

Cad Bane is a very skilled bounty hunter. Bounty hunters track down wanted people for money. This money is called a bounty.

He blows things up, and, above all else, he enjoys a good fight.

Cad Bane is armed and dangerous. He carries around two blasters and has breathing tubes fixed into his cheeks.

Cad Bane also wears a special pair of rocket boots, so he can take off whenever he wants.

Wrist Weapons

Cad Bane's wrist glove has cable launchers, communication devices, and non-lethal stunners.

Cad Bane usually works alone.
But if the job is big enough,
he calls on his fellow bounty
hunters to help him.

Once, Bane hired a team of battle-hardened bounty hunters to help raid the Senate Building. Let's meet them all.

Aurra Sing is a mysterious bounty hunter with pale white skin, dark sunken eyes, and long fingers. She has two pistols and a rifle.

While Cad Bane attacks the Senate, Aurra Sing hides nearby. As the rest of Bane's team appear, Sing shoots at the Senate guards.

Sing's Style
Aurra's head is bald except for one long tuft of red-brown hair.

Bane's team of bounty hunters step out of their ships, one by one.

Fast Shooter

Alama has rough, wrinkled skin.
He is quick with a blaster.

First is Shahan Alama.

He is a type of alien called

a Weequay (pronounced

WEE-KWAY).

Robonino is another member of Cad Bane's team.

He is an alien with fishy features.

His backpack is full of useful tools.

Wrecking Kit
Robonino carries special tools to destroy electronic systems and set explosive devices.

Robonino's job is to shut down the Senate's power so no one can enter or exit the building.

When Anakin tries to stop him, Robonino zaps him with electricity.

These two vile villains are
BX-series droid commandos.
They are smart and very tough.

Senate Guards

Senate guards
protect the people
inside the Senate.
They wear rugged,
blue armor.

The two droids disguise themselves as Senate guards. They help protect Cad Bane.

Completing the gang are two very
dangerous IG-86 sentinel droids.
The first sentinel droid searches
the Senate for Anakin Skywalker.

But even a smart and fast
sentinel droid does not stand
a chance against a great Jedi
Knight such as Anakin.

Cad Bane has kidnapped some Senators and bargained for a dangerous prisoner to be released.

Ziro the Hutt
Ziro is a crime lord who was imprisoned for his part in a kidnapping.

He sends the second sentinel droid
to collect the prisoner.
The prisoner is called Ziro the Hutt.

Cad Bane enjoys difficult missions. When Darth Sidious asks him to break into the Jedi Temple, Bane knows it will be a tough challenge. Bane agrees to do the job, but he demands a high fee and a new ship!

Jedi Temple

The Jedi Temple is the headquarters of the Jedi Order. It is where the Jedi meet and train.

Bane asks Cato Parasitti
to help him on his mission.

Cato disguises herself as
a Jedi and turns off the
Temple's security systems.

But Ahsoka realizes
that the Jedi is really Cato.
Cato fights Ahsoka, and Cato's
face changes back to normal.

Cato Parasitti
Cato can change her
features to look like
someone else.

Bane also uses a techno-service
droid called Todo 360.
Bane and Todo 360 rocket
up to the roof of the Jedi Temple.
Todo 360 cuts a hole to get in.

But Bane has a deadly
surprise for Todo 360.
He puts a bomb in the
droid and under cover of
the explosion, Bane escapes.

Cad Bane is a cunning fighter. When Anakin and Ahsoka confront Bane on board a spaceship, he turns off the gravity.

All of a sudden Anakin and Ahsoka start to float upward. They have to avoid Bane's blaster shots while floating in the air!

Ahsoka catches Cad Bane by grabbing his arm and flipping him to the ground.
But Bane uses a weapon on his wrist to hit Ahsoka with an energy blast.

Once again, Cad Bane escapes capture, somehow slipping away. Who knows where he will appear next time!

Quiz!

1. What is the name of this feared bounty hunter?

2. Do you know the name of this bounty hunter?

3. Who protects the Senate?

4. Who is Ziro the Hutt?

5. Who helps Cad Bane on his mission?

6. Who stops Cad Bane?

Answers: 1. Cad Bane, 2. Aurra Sing, 3. The Senate guards, 4. A crime lord, 5. Cato Parasitti, 6. Ahsoka